Emergence of a Modern Dwelling:
Richard Neutra's Hassrick House

ORO EDITIONS
Publishers of Architecture, Art, and Design

www.oroeditions.com
info@oroeditions.com

Published by ORO Editions

Editors: Suzanne Singletary and Suzanna Barucco
Copy Editor: David Breiner
ORO printing coordination: Jake Anderson

Book design: Pablo Mandel
www.circularstudio.com

Texts set in Futura and TT Norms

10 9 8 7 6 5 4 3 2 1   FIRST EDITION

Library of Congress data available upon request.
World Rights: Available

ISBN: 978-1-954081-17-8

Color Separations and Printing: ORO Group Ltd.
Printed in China.

International Distribution: www.oroeditions.com/distribution

ORO Editions makes a continuous effort to minimize the overall carbon footprint of its publications.
As part of this goal, ORO Editions, in association with Global ReLeaf, arranges to plant trees to
replace those used in the manufacturing of the paper produced for its books. Global ReLeaf is an
international campaign run by American Forests, one of the world's oldest nonprofit conservation
organizations. Global ReLeaf is American Forests' education and action program that helps
individuals, organizations, agencies, and corporations improve the local and global environment by
planting and caring for trees.

Emergence of a Modern Dwelling: Richard Neutra's Hassrick House

Edited by Suzanne Singletary and Suzanna Barucco

With contributions by Andrew Hart, Alison Eberhardt, Allee Davis, Shannon McLain, Hussain Aljoher

CENTER FOR
THE PRESERVATION
OF MODERNISM

CABE – COLLEGE
OF ARCHITECTURE
& THE BUILT ENVIRONMENT

Jefferson
Thomas Jefferson University

ORO EDITIONS, NOVATO, CALIFORNIA

This publication is dedicated to all of the students who have tirelessly researched and documented the Hassrick House and continue to serve as its stewards, and to George Acosta and John Hauser, without whose generosity this story might not have been written.

Contents

Executive Letter

Sponsored by Thomas Jefferson University's Center for the Preservation of Modernism, the publication of *Emergence of a Modern Dwelling: Richard Neutra's Hassrick House* fulfills a key goal of the Center—to spotlight architecture and sites of the modern movement. The Center for the Preservation of Modernism builds upon Jefferson's legacy in undergraduate preservation education, which dates back to the first introductory course taught in 1997. From these nascent beginnings evolved a twelve-credit minor and then a twenty-four credit concentration, both developed in response to student demand. More recently, student interest in the emergent role of preservation in broader issues of economic development, sustainability, adaptive reuse and main street revitalization contributed to the launch of the Master of Science in Historic Preservation in 2019. Jefferson's 2017 purchase of the Hassrick House (1959–1961), one of the few East Coast residences designed by Richard Neutra and an exemplar of mid-century modern architecture, strengthened our conviction that this period should be one curricular focus of the graduate program and an area in which Jefferson can make a significant contribution.

Modern buildings and sites represent the next preservation frontier as these buildings age. The Hassrick House epitomizes the stylistic features associated with the modern movement—its flat roof, wide expanses of single-pane windows and novel materials by definition raise questions relative to conservation, sustainability, and integrity, while also insinuating a need for an expanded definition of the practice of preservation itself. This period presents unique challenges in terms of condition assessment, material restoration, structural stabilization and curtain-wall facade retrofitting, while embodying distinctive social, cultural and philosophical meanings. The overarching goal of the modernist aesthetic was to enhance human life through enlightened ways of dwelling, in the broadest possible sense. Neutra aimed to concretize that promise in the Hassrick House.

The mission of the Center for the Preservation of Modernism is to support research that addresses the protection and conservation of these structures, as well as to develop an archive on modernist architecture to serve as a resource for scholars and students. Importantly, the Center promotes advocacy and serves as a meeting ground for the larger preservation community, offering lectures and symposia that address pressing issues facing modern structures and sites. The inaugural event in 2019 featured Dr. Theodore Prudon, eminent architect, preservationist, author and founding president of Docomomo US (Documentation and Conservation - Modern Movement). The event drew over two hundred attendees to hear Dr. Prudon and to visit Neutra's Hassrick House, guided in expert docent tours provided by our dedicated Historic Preservation students. Our partnerships with the Bauhaus (Hochshule Anhalt Dessau, Germany) and the Giuseppe Terragni Archive in Lake Como, Italy broaden our scope well beyond regional boundaries. The Center for the Preservation of Modernism positions Jefferson at the forefront in preserving our modern heritage, nationally and internationally.

This publication reflects the continuous dedication and myriad contributions by Jefferson faculty, staff and students. Special thanks go to Andrew Hart, who initiated Jefferson's relationship with the Hassrick House and continues to shepherd our students; to Suzanna Barucco, co-author and editor, whose rigorous scholarship and lucid vision shaped every part of this publication; and to Alison Eberhardt, dedicated associate and collaborator, whose knowledge of the Hassrick House and skills in research and coordination were indispensable. Our understanding of the building and the visual impact of the book owe a great debt to Shannon McLain's expert architectural renderings and to the excellent photographic essays contributed by Allee Davis and Hussain Aljoher. Graphic designer Pablo Mandel accomplished the daunting task of translating the work of multiple contributors into a clear and visually compelling book. Members of the CABE faculty generously offered their expertise, insight and support, including David Breiner, James Doerfler, Concetta Dragani, Rob Fleming, Grace Ong Yan, Lorraine Schnabel, and James Querry. I would also like to thank the Physical Plant staff, especially Thomas Becker, Matthew Gulbicki and Stefanie Karp, the Safety and Security staff, librarian Sarah Slate, archivist Kelsey Dunkerken, and CABE's Christianna Fail and Sarah Bott for their ongoing assistance and support. Particular thanks go to Barbara Klinkhammer, Dean of the College of Architecture & the Built Environment, for her encouragement, leadership and vision, and to Mark Tykocinski, MD, Provost and Executive Vice President for Academic Affairs, Thomas Jefferson University, for his generosity funding this project. Lastly, to Hal and Jonathan Sawyer, John Hauser, and George Acosta for sharing their experiences and memories—thanks.

Suzanne Singletary, Ph.D.
Director, The Center for the Preservation of Modernism
Director, M.S. Historic Preservation

Introduction

In the East Falls neighborhood of Philadelphia, just beyond the northern boundary of Thomas Jefferson University's campus, stands the Hassrick House, designed by celebrated architect and icon of mid-century modernism, Richard Neutra. The residence occupies its original three acres on Cherry Lane, a narrow road accessible from School House Lane. Construction of the house began in the early months of 1958 and was largely complete by February of 1959—complete enough at least for Barbara and Kenneth Hassrick and their three young sons to move in. Building continued well into 1960 with the original footprint enlarged to include a Neutra-designed garage addition.[1] A second building phase began in 1961 with the addition of a studio wing to the rear, designed by Irwin Stein, an up-and-coming Philadelphia architect working in the mid-century modern style.[2] Sliding privacy panels by well-known Bucks County, Pennsylvania, craftsman, George Nakashima, were installed in the centrally positioned kitchen in 1961, further enhancing the building's design caché. Often described as an East Coast interpretation of California Modernism, Neutra's original schema, combined with Stein's compatibly styled addition, is one of only three dwellings designed by Neutra within the city limits of Philadelphia, earning the Hassrick House its listing in the Philadelphia Register of Historic Places in 2009.

Thomas Jefferson University's relationship with the house began in the summer of 2015 when Andrew Hart, Assistant Professor of Architecture in the College of Architecture & the Built Environment (CABE), initiated a series of summer courses to study the house. The first multidisciplinary group of students engaged in architectural survey (on site measuring), drawing and photography. Subsequent summer courses refined the architectural drawings, following the Historic American Buildings Survey (HABS) and Historic American Landscape Survey (HALS) standards, and generated an energy audit and LiDAR scan of the building.[3] Yet another student cohort undertook documentary research to uncover the history of the house and its occupants. This latter group confirmed another suspected connection to the Nakashima Studio, upon finding a receipt in the woodworking studio's archives for a credenza purchased for the house by the Hassricks in 1959.

By all accounts, then owners George Acosta and John Hauser welcomed the students with open arms.[4] These classes were, in fact, a mutually supportive collaboration among the students and George and

John, as they were known. Neutra's architecture and his relationship with the Hassricks—particularly Barbara who, as the primary correspondent, emerged as the client voice while the house was being designed—captured the hearts, minds, and imaginations of everyone who engaged with the house. As one student recalled, "We have all gotten swept away in the stories unfolding from our research."[5]

In 2017, when John Hauser's employment required the couple to relocate, Jefferson stepped in to purchase the site. George and John sold the property to the university with the understanding that the house would continue to be used for educational purposes. In George's words, "I had come to realize that the students can be the future custodians of that home. They can be the eyes. They can be the archives. In a way, it becomes all of ours to share..."[6] In fulfillment of that vision, the Hassrick House is the recognized public face of Jefferson's Center for the Preservation of Modernism. The house continues to serve as a resource for historic preservation, architecture, interior design, construction management, sustainable design, and landscape architecture students, just as George and John had hoped.

This publication celebrates Jefferson student work on the Hassrick House to date, shedding light on Neutra's design process, his collaboration with his clients, and the unsung role of Pennsylvania architect Thaddeus Longstreth who served as Neutra's representative throughout the design and construction stages. The Hassrick House tells a saga of design, dwelling, neglect, restoration, and reinvention today as a laboratory for learning.

TIMELINE

1956
Ken and Barbara Hassrick meet Neutra and begin correspondence

1958
Construction begins on Neutra's original design

1960
Completion of two-story garage addition designed by Neutra

1961
Construction of Irwin Stein studio addition; George Nakashima-designed kitchen panels are installed

1963
Hassricks sell house to Henry and Grace Sawyer

2002
The last Sawyer, son Hal, moves out of the Hassrick House

2002–2006
John and Amy McCoubrey own the Hassrick House

2006–2008
The house is vacant during the ownership of developer John Capoferri, and eventually foreclosed by the bank

2008
George Acosta and John Hauser purchase the Hassrick House; begin restoration

2015–2017
George Acosta and John Hauser share their house with students

2017
Philadelphia University (later Thomas Jefferson University) purchases house

2019
The 'Fourth Cohort' of students designs an exhibit for the inaugural program of The Center for the Preservation of Modernism at Thomas Jefferson University

Hassrick House, perspective sketch by Richard Neutra, believed to have
been sent to Thaddeus Longstreth 3 March 1957, along with plan options
A, B and C. Thaddeus Longstreth Collection, The Architectural Archives,
University of Pennsylvania.

CHAPTER 1

Richard Joseph Neutra 1892–1970

I try to make a house like a flowerpot,
in which you can root something and out of which family life will bloom.

–Richard Neutra[1]

Richard Neutra was one of the most influential architects of the 20th century, renowned for his role in introducing the International Style of Europe into American architecture and for helping to define modernism in the United States and abroad. His wide-ranging portfolio includes residences, schools, multi-family housing, institutional and commercial buildings. Located primarily in Southern California where his practice was based, Neutra's signature designs are also sprinkled throughout the United States, across Europe, and one far-afield site in Asia.[2] In addition to the nearly one hundred residences designed and built between 1927 and 1969 for the temperate California climate, Neutra's indoor-outdoor, open plan houses can also be found in several East Coast states, including Maryland, New York, Delaware, and Pennsylvania.[3]

Neutra's design ideals were disseminated through his many published projects in specialty magazines, such as *Architectural Forum* and *Interiors*, and also through his own articles, books, and speaking engagements, garnering the attention of admirers, adherents, and clients alike.[4] In the Forward to the catalogue of the ground-breaking 1932 Museum of Modern Art (MoMA) exhibit, *Modern Architecture: International*

Exhibition, MoMA Director Alfred H. Barr, Jr. wrote, "Principally because of his writing the Austrian-born Neutra is, among American architects, second only to [Frank Lloyd] Wright in his international reputation."[5] The 15 August 1949 *TIME* magazine cover and feature article on Neutra—with the provocative heading, "What will the neighbors think?"—extended his name recognition beyond architecture circles, popularizing his bold style and theories with the American public, as did regular feature articles in such mainstream publications as *Better Homes and Gardens* and *Ladies Home Journal*.[6] (Figure 1.1)

In 1911, Neutra enrolled in the architecture program at the Vienna University of Technology, a decision sparked by an early interest in the work of Austrian Secessionist Otto Wagner. Wagner's widely read 1896 text, *Modern Architecture,* helped shape a modernist aesthetic suited to contemporary lifestyles utilizing new materials and methods of construction.[7] During this formative period Neutra met two individuals who would influence his professional path, Viennese architect and polemicist, Adolf Loos (1870-1933), and fellow classmate and future collaborator, Rudolf M. Schindler (1887-1953). Neutra entered the orbit of Loos at a time when the elder architect was rejecting the Secessionists in favor of an architecture stripped of applied ornamentation. Loos's radical theories were encapsulated in his seminal 1908 essay, *Ornament and Crime*, and were later adopted by the Bauhaus and other modernists. Like Neutra, Schindler was also a follower of Loos's architectural theories and absorbed their mentor's enthusiasm for American culture, specifically the work of Frank Lloyd Wright. Trained as an artist and engineer, Schindler turned to architecture at Loos's urging and emigrated to the United States in 1914. In the employ of Wright, Schindler travelled to Los Angeles to oversee construction of the Hollyhock House and decided to stay, opening his own practice there in 1921.[8]

Early in his career, Neutra worked in the office of expressionist modern architect, Erich Mendelsohn, and in 1923 contributed to the firm's award-winning competition entry for a commercial center in Haifa, Palestine. Neutra's first foray into domestic design dates to his employ in Mendelsohn's practice. From 1921-1923, he designed ten detached houses in Zehlendorf, a west Berlin suburb, that display on a small scale what would become iconic features of his California houses—flat white facades, ribbon windows, cantilevered balconies, and interpenetrating interior spaces.[9] Upon completion of the Zehlendorf project, Neutra left Europe and moved to the United States, finding employment first with the notable firm of Holabird and Roche in Chicago—site of works by Louis Sullivan and Wright, both of whom Neutra met in 1924—and later with Wright at Taliesin in Spring Green, Wisconsin. Neutra reconnected with Schindler when he moved to Los Angeles in 1925. The two briefly had a shared practice before Neutra left in 1930 for a yearlong trip to Europe, Japan, and China during which he met exemplars of the modernist vanguard, including Le Corbusier, Alvar Aalto, Walter Gropius, and Ludwig Mies van der Rohe, and taught as a guest critic at the Dessau Bauhaus for a month.[10]

Success seemed to follow Neutra. Soon after his arrival in California, he was awarded a significant commission, the design of the Lovell House for Leah and Philip Lovell, a naturopathic physician, in Los Angeles who advocated natural healing and preventive healthcare.[11] (Figure 1.2) Built in 1929, the three-story Lovell "Health" House, as it was also called, was an early example of the International Style in the United States. Its streamlined aesthetic, airy structure and hovering, overlapping planes synthesized principles developed by both Le Corbusier and Wright as absorbed and interpreted by Neutra, who incorporated areas for exercise, sports and outdoor living in synchrony with Lovell's theories. Notable for a structural system of steel columns, beams, pilotis, and tension cables that tether the house to the side of a cliff, the house appears to levitate above its mountain setting. Widely acclaimed, the Lovell House was the first documented steel-framed house in America; its pronounced "machine aesthetic" and daring integration with a dramatic, though challenging, site exemplified Neutra's interest in structural experimentation and new technologies.[12] (Figure 1.3) A debut tour of the building drew approximately 15,000 visitors and solidified Neutra's status as a master of American modernism.

The Lovell House marked a turning point in Neutra's career, and no doubt contributed to his being selected to be among those featured in the aforementioned 1932 MoMA exhibit, *Modern Architecture: International Exhibition*. Curated by future architect Philip Johnson and architectural historian Henry-Russell Hitchcock, the exhibition popularized the label, International Style, and identified this approach through the works of "progressive architects [who] have converged to form a genuinely new style which is rapidly spreading throughout the world. Both in appearance and structure, this style is peculiar to the twentieth century

1.1

1.1 *TIME*, 15 August 1949
From TIME©1949 TIME USA LLC.
All rights reserved. Used under license.

1.2

and is as fundamentally original as the Greek or Byzantine or Gothic."[13] The authors formulated the principal identifiers of the International Style, namely, the integration of structure and design, simplified geometry, and lack of applied ornamentation. Moreover, the exhibit travelled to eleven American cities after leaving New York and showcased Neutra alongside such European luminaries as Le Corbusier, Gropius, Mies, and J.J.P. Oud, among others.

Neutra's work was distinguished beyond the bounds of the International Style, however, by a theory he called bio-realism, a belief in the overriding importance of integrating architecture and nature to benefit mankind. In his 1954 anthology, entitled *Survival through Design*, Neutra argued that architects "must still design living space, and a current environment for the race, so that the neurological salubrious agents of nature outside are freely admitted and kept active to as great an extent as possible."[14] For Neutra, harmonious design could mediate between the individual and the deleterious state of civilization to effect spaces that were intrinsically therapeutic. Through his writings and projects, Neutra promoted the architect's social responsibility to design life-enhancing spaces through their intimate connection to light and nature.

Neutra's amalgam of Bauhaus modernism with Wright's attention to the specifics of climate and topography is vividly expressed in one of his most celebrated works, the 1946 Kaufmann Desert House, in Palm Springs, California. (Figure 1.4) Designed as a winter retreat for Pittsburgh millionaire Edgar J. Kaufmann—who ten years earlier commissioned Wright to design his country home in Bear Run, Pennsylvania, resulting in Fallingwater—the house perfectly marries the minimalist International Style with the surrounding desert terrain and mountain setting. As with the Lovell House, the lightweight steel structure and hovering horizontal roof planes give the Kaufmann House an airy feeling and understated aesthetic. Floor-to-ceiling, plate glass window walls can fully open to merge inside and outside, allowing interior spaces to bleed out onto porches and patios, removing the barriers between house and landscape. A building of transparency and illumination, the Kaufmann Desert House epitomizes Neutra's ideal of bio-realism; his belief that architecture can be a balm to both body and mind through a visceral connection to the rhythms of nature. (Figure 1.5)

Neutra's conviction that architecture can play a significant role in both the physical and psychological well-being of its occupants stems from his early training and influences. The reformist, social agenda of European modernists, including Loos and Le Corbusier, and their belief in architecture's healing power were deleted in the MoMA exhibition that foregrounded stylistic features, but their example serves as a backdrop to Neutra's formulation of biorealism, as does the exemplary work of Wright. To these models he layered his life-long allegiance to the theories of psychologists Wilhelm Wundt, Wilhelm Reich, and particularly Sigmund Freud, and current notions of health, fitness and preventive medicine, as espoused by Lovell.[15] Neutra became known for synthesizing architecture and health, attracting clients desirous of his life-enhancing, healing environments. The efficacy of Neutra's design methodology is attested by the testimonials of his many satisfied clients.[16]

1.3

1.2 Richard Neutra, Lovell House, 1928. Los Feliz neighborhood, Los Angeles, California. Richard and Dion Neutra papers (Collection 1179). Library Special Collections, Charles E. Young Research Library, UCLA.

1.3 Richard Neutra, Lovell House, 1928. Los Feliz neighborhood, Los Angeles, California. Richard and Dion Neutra papers (Collection 1179). Library Special Collections, Charles E. Young Research Library, UCLA.

1.4

1.4 Richard Neutra, Kaufmann Desert House,
Palm Springs, California, 1998.
© J. Paul Getty Trust. Getty Research
Institute, Los Angeles (2004.R.10).

1.5

Neutra's social philosophy and modernist aesthetic made him an obvious choice for editor John Entenza's Case Study Program, sponsored by *Art & Architecture* magazine between 1945 and 1966. Entenza challenged major modernist architects to design low-cost, standardized housing prototypes for the California climate, in response to the post-World War II residential building boom. Neutra contributed four designs, although only Case Study House #20 the Bailey House, was built in 1948 and published in the December issue of *Art & Architecture*, accompanied by Neutra's explanatory essay.[17] (Figure 1.6) This low budget, two-bedroom, rectangular pavilion, intended for a young family, allowed the architect to prove that "smallness may be stretched by skill of space arrangement and by borrowing space from the outdoors in several directions."[18] In a series of signature gestures, Neutra evoked expansive space by fronting the entire width of one side of the house with sliding glass window walls that open to patios, garden and ocean views; controlling the intensity of natural and artificial lighting; and contrasting the grains and colors of wood finishes within the interior to evoke a spectrum of moods. To save costs, Neutra inserted a prefabricated utility core of plumbing and heating equipment between the kitchen and the bathroom. Spatial units are grouped, based upon the needs of the users.

Ultimately, he wrote, "design must, in the stages of realization, penetrate the minds of the householders to make the whole a success."[19] Stuart Bailey, owner of Case Study House #20, described the experience of the house as one that, "does not just sit here passively. I feel that it acts on me in a most beneficial manner. It draws me to it."[20] In many respects, Case Study House #20 is a harbinger of the spatial and budgetary solutions Neutra would bring to bear a decade later in the design of the Hassrick House.

1.6

1.6 Richard Neutra, Case Study House
#20, Bailey House, Los Angeles, California.
Julius Shulman, photographer (1948)
© J. Paul Getty Trust. Getty Research Institute,
Los Angeles (2004.R.10).

2021

Large Format Black and White Photographs
Allee Davis and Alison Eberhardt

1.7

1.8

1.7 Previous spread: View to the southwest.

1.8 Detail view of the Bethayres block wall adjacent to the main entrance.

1.9 View to the east from the dining area toward the living room fireplace wall. The entrance foyer is behind the fireplace wall.

1.9

1.10

1.10 View to the southeast. Note the panels designed by George Nakashima and installed in 1961 to enclose the kitchen. The original workroom is in the background at right photo.

1.11 View to the north from the kitchen area.

1.11

1.12

1.13

1.14

1.12 View to the northeast in the Stein Addition.

1.13 View to the southwest toward the kitchen from the main entrance foyer. The bedrooms are down the corridor seen at right photo.

1.14 View to the southeast in the original recreation room. The Stein Addition can be seen through the windows beyond.

1.15 View to the northwest in the original master bedroom.

1.15

Hassrick House, perspective sketch by Richard Neutra, believed to have been sent to Thaddeus Longstreth 3 March 1957, along with plan options A, B and C. Courtesy Jonathan Sawyer.

CHAPTER 2

The House of the Hassricks

This is to say, the house must: 1/work efficiently, 2/pleasure the eye, 3/comfort the soul, and 4/warm the heart.

–Barbara Hassrick[1]

I t is not known what prompted the Hassricks to seek out Neutra in 1956 to design their residence. One source suggests that Barbara Hassrick was inspired after reading about the architect's work in the 1949 feature article in *TIME* magazine.[2] (See Figure 1.1) The *TIME* article did highlight Neutra's skill in designing houses in various price brackets, including for those on a limited budget, and his practice of customizing each dwelling to suit the occupants. Both traits would have appealed to the Hassricks. The young couple was on a budget, and while they frequently expressed admiration for Neutra and deference to his design proposals, they also had very specific ideas of their own. By the 1950s, however, Neutra's reputation as a modernist architect was well established and his work widely published. The Hassricks could have seen his extensive coverage in *Interiors* between 1949 and 1956, as well as in other popular magazines of the period. Closer to home, in April 1956, Neutra visited Philadelphia at the invitation of the local chapter of the American Institute of Architects (AIA) to consult on potential sites for a new sports arena, and to provide input on a controversial housing project in the Northeast section of the

2.1

2.1 The Hassricks might have sent this image in response to Neutra's request for family photographs in February 1957. Pictured from left, Jeremy Fox, Jonathan Fox, Barbara Hassrick, her father Edwin Burk Estabrook, her mother Dorothy Parker Estabrook, and Kenneth Hassrick. Courtesy Jonathan Fox.

city, supported by the City Planning Commission. Neutra's advice was valued due to his international renown and experience with both large-scale projects and housing.[3]

Our understanding of the design process and the architect/client relationship is largely told through the, at times daily, correspondence between Neutra, his associate Thaddeus Longstreth, and the Hassricks. Neutra's commitment to biorealism permeates these letters, in particular his efforts to tailor the house to the Hassricks' requirements. The architect was known to ask his residential clients for a diary of daily activities for each family member, an assignment that would be supplemented by extensive interviews and photographs.[4] (Figure 2.1) Through this process, Neutra gained insight into the day-to-day needs of his clients which allowed him to imbue his designs with indoor/outdoor environments intended to enhance daily comfort, nurture personal fulfillment, and promote familial harmony. Neutra likened this process to psychotherapy, writing: "An architect producing by proper means of rapport with the client's aspirations and expressed or half-expressed need is acting very closely to...the procedure of a psychiatrist."[5] Like Louis Sullivan and Frank Lloyd Wright, Neutra viewed a building as "organic," a living organism and work of nature whose form evolves from need and yields a symbiotic relationship with the users. By choosing Neutra as architect, the Hassricks were not only endorsing a modernist aesthetic, but also embracing a "modern" lifestyle.

The letters suggest that both Kenneth and Barbara Hassrick were equally engaged in the design of the house, although, as the primary correspondent it is Barbara's voice that forcefully emerges. Ellen Barbara Estabrook was born on February 15, 1921 to Edwin Burk and Dorothy Parker Estabrook and grew up in the Germantown neighborhood of Philadelphia. Barbara, as she was known, attended the Stevens School in Philadelphia and had her coming out as a debutante at the age of 17.[6] She earned a BA in Philosophy from Connecticut College in 1943. A first marriage to Roy Fox, Jr. ended in divorce.[7] Kenneth Hassrick was an artist primarily producing "works of abstract metal sculpture, wax, clay and plaster" which he exhibited with regularity, and to some acclaim, in Philadelphia galleries.[8] He was acknowledged later in his career for his "evocative semi-abstract paintings of the female figure."[9] His other passion was collecting and restoring classic cars, particularly Bugattis. The couple married in 1953, and as a wedding gift received three acres of land on Cherry Lane in East

Falls from Barbara's parents, a portion of a parcel the senior Estabrooks had purchased in 1940.

By the time that the Hassricks contacted Neutra, the architect had already designed two residences in nearby Montgomery County, Pennsylvania, the Cohen House (1954) in Wyndmoor, and the Miller House (1955) in West Norriton Township.[10] What brought Neutra to the Philadelphia market may have been his reputation, but his work in the region was surely fostered by his relationship with local architect Thaddeus Longstreth (1908-1997). Longstreth, a native of Ohio, earned a bachelor's degree from Yale and a graduate degree in architecture from Princeton University. He worked as a draftsman for Neutra in Southern California from 1945 to 1947. When he returned to the East Coast, he worked in the offices of two notable Philadelphia modernists, Oscar Stonorov (1947-1948) and Vincent Kling (1948-1949). Longstreth established an independent practice in Washington Crossing, Pennsylvania, in 1950.[11] In addition to maintaining his own practice, Longstreth served as Neutra's representative for the Hassrick House and for all of Neutra's Delaware Valley projects.[12] One can imagine the value of this relationship to the California architect. Typical of his role as intermediary between Neutra and his clients, Longstreth participated in the earliest discussions with the Hassricks and no doubt aided in allaying the couple's initial concerns about Neutra's distance from the project.[13] Longstreth was not only able to present Neutra's architectural designs to the Hassricks, but could also respond to practical questions from the architect regarding local building traditions, codes, materials, and construction costs.[14]

Neutra visited the Hassricks' "lovely lot" on Cherry Lane in late November or early December of 1956. The meeting of minds between the Hassricks and Neutra is evident in their earliest correspondence.[15] Writing with a list of their ideas for the house, Barbara enthused, "We are so convinced that your ideas of a home are also ours that we found that we kept saying 'Oh, don't put that down, he *knows*.'" Yet, the letter includes three pages of detailed notes on the Hassricks' requirements, from the pitch of the roof—"We would like a roof with a single pitch rather than flat top if not too many $ involved"—to materials—the recreation room "floor should be asphalt tile, walls need not be finished at present."[16] Plus, terraces should be "convenient to kitchen…also if possible to bedrooms and recreation room," and the living room should have cork floors and a "free

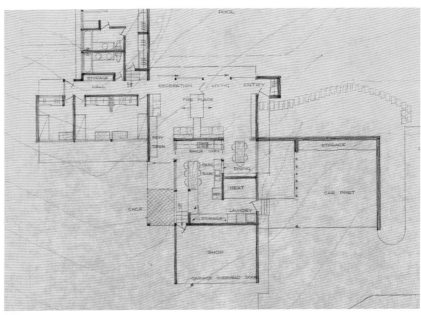

2.2

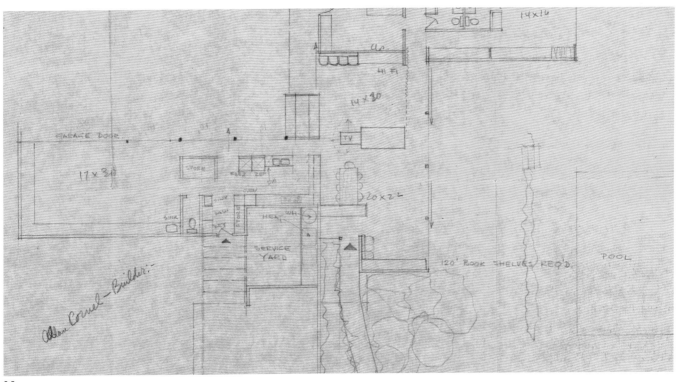

2.3

standing fireplace in the dining room that Ken will design." Other amenities on their list included radiant heat in the floors, wood for ceilings or walls of solid panels, a carport and a shop for Ken. It was the Hassricks who requested that the house be built of pink Bethayres block, a concrete masonry block manufactured by the Bethayres Concrete Products Company in Bethayres, Pennsylvania, approximately ten miles north of Philadelphia. Above all, the couple wanted the house to exude a "warm, friendly, *gemütlich* feeling, expressed somehow in the clean fine style of the early Japanese," be easy to maintain and require minimal housework.[17]

Barbara Hassrick also had very specific ideas for the kitchen, telling Neutra, "On this I could write a book."[18] She admitted that she liked "a great big old-fashioned kitchen that's stylish enough to entertain in, but this seems to be not the thing in a modern house."[19] A visit to Longstreth's residence in Washington Crossing helped Barbara clarify her concept of the "modern" kitchen as "...adjoining and open to [the] dining area, but [with a] sliding wall to close [it] off—Mr. Longstreth's is just about IT..." She further added her wish for a counter between the kitchen and the dining area that would operate, with "doors on both sides," to allow dishes to be passed through between the two spaces but without seeing the entire kitchen.[20] Barbara desired the "modern" openness between the kitchen and dining areas while still maintaining each space's "old-fashioned," separate functional identity.

In one of his early plans for the house, Neutra indicated an eat-in, relatively self-contained kitchen adjacent to, but separate from, the dining area that was accessed through a side doorway. (Figure 2.2) In later iterations, the dining room is the designated eating area and directly adjoins the kitchen, interconnecting these two spaces, but both separated from the living room by an open fireplace wall. (Figure 2.3) As built, the kitchen and living areas all interconnect. The living and dining areas share an open rectangular space with the fireplace, now moved to one end of the room. The kitchen flows into the living areas, its permeable border defined by a counter and a line of suspended cabinets. (Figure 2.4)

After submitting several proposed solutions to the kitchen conundrum and extensive back and forth negotiations, in a letter dated March 8, 1957 Longstreth reported to Neutra that the "Hassricks think our arrangement here at the Crossing is ideal." Moreover, in Longstreth's retelling, the proscribed openness in the relationship between the kitchen and living area

2.2–2.3 Proposed plans of the Hassrick House, believed to have been sent from Richard Neutra to Thaddeus Longstreth in March 1957. Thaddeus Longstreth Collection, The Architectural Archives, University of Pennsylvania.

2.4

forecasts an idyllic picture of husband and wife in the same room, while she cooks dinner and he lounges "in an easy chair after a hard day at the office." Longstreth further recounted the Hassricks' conviction that the "kitchen should be the focal point of the house."[21] However, in contrast to this everyday domestic scenario, when entertaining, Barbara preferred the flexibility of closing off the kitchen with what she described as "removable walls."[22] She concluded that the "best compromise is a kitchen that is open to the dining area (which is part of the living room) with a 4 stool snack bar dividing it off and a sliding wall of some kind."[23]

The malleable boundaries envisioned by Barbara, between kitchen and dining areas, allowing either interconnecting or separate options, remained elusive and unsatisfactory. In 1959, the Hassricks had commissioned George Nakashima (1905-1990), New Hope, Pennsylvania based architect and furniture designer, to create a credenza for the dining area.[24] (Figure 2.5) They turned to Nakashima again to resolve the long-standing open/closed kitchen issue. In April 1961, Barbara sent Longstreth photos of Nakashima's design of movable walnut panels, inserted within a thin wooden frame and positioned between the upper cabinets and counter. When fully extended, these simple sliding screens achieved the desired separation between kitchen and dining/living spaces. She proclaimed the Nakashima panels to be the "final arrangement of the kitchen closing off problem...we're real pleased with the functional aspects, and it looks quite Japanezy and nice."[25] (See Figures 1.10 and 3.2).

As early as January 1957, the overall layout of the house had been established, although for several months myriad elements were debated, negotiated, and changed, in part due to the constraints of the Hassricks' allotted budget. In a letter dated January 14th, Neutra first broached the subject of cost, writing that, "your planned budget may be quite tight to include all of your ideas," and insisting that while some items might need to be postponed, the goal was "an integrated entity not to be marred by a lot of afterthoughts and patch-ups," but still meeting essential programmatic requirements.[26] In response, Barbara broke down their current "financial calculations" into two categories: what the Hassricks could install themselves during and/or after construction, and what would require professional help but could wait until after the house was built.[27] Longstreth's suggestion that construction of the carport and shop be postponed to save money elicited the first note of surprise, disappointment, and

2.4 Previous Page. Hassrick House circa 1960. View to the east from the dining area toward the living area. Thaddeus Longstreth Collection, The Architectural Archives, University of Pennsylvania. Photograph by Lawrence Williams.

2.5 Hassrick House circa 1960. View to the south from the dining area toward the kitchen. The workshop, two steps above the main house level, was behind the door in the background. Note the Nakashima credenza purchased by the Hassricks in 1959 at right photo. Lawrence S. Williams Collection; Athenaeum of Philadelphia.

2.5

even annoyance from the couple.[28] The Hassricks did ultimately relent and accepted a reduced footprint, thanks largely to the intercession of Longstreth. Neutra advised Longstreth to "please gently correct" the Hassricks' mistaken expectations regarding the capabilities of their limited budget.[29] Dutifully, Longstreth reported to Neutra that he explained to the Hassricks "the consequences and chain reactions caused by changes in plan," and that construction costs are "predictable only by occult powers."[30]

Still, Barbara Hassrick expressed additional concerns about reducing square footage due to lack of storage in a house without a basement—a cellar was unequivocally nixed by Neutra—and about potential maintenance issues caused by a flat roof in the wet Mid-Atlantic climate—Longstreth reassured her that a flat roof would not present maintenance problems.[31]

2.6

One recurring item of discussion was the location of space allotted to the family pets, principally "Willie," the monkey, whose cage finally found a warm, draft-free spot by an interior kitchen wall.[32] To save money Neutra suggested interior level changes to avoid grading expenses by placing the master bedroom suite "two or three steps lower...and the workshop...two or three steps higher than the main living area," adjustments approved by the Hassricks.[33] (Figures 2.5 and 2.6)

In March 1957, Neutra sent three potential schemes to Longstreth to present to the Hassricks, labeled Plan A, Plan B, and Plan C, each in descending order in terms of scale and cost.[34] While initially selecting Plan C, the most "reduced version, keeping the most desirable features," after a three-hour meeting with Longstreth, the Hassricks ultimately chose Plan A, "the most ample solution." Approval, however, included a list of further changes—closing off the recreation room from the living room, constructing removable walls between each of the three children's rooms, and pre-fabricated fireplaces for both living room and recreation room. The most contentious change was the request for a "swimming pool a natural shape with a rock garden...on the south side, not oriented to living area since in winter it is barren to look at and a frozen asset..."[35] In Neutra's California residences, the swimming pool serves as what he described as a "million dollar mirror" year round, enjoying pride of place parallel to vast expanses of window walls in primary living spaces. To retain some of the jewel-like reflectivity of water, Neutra reluctantly placed the pool on the south side—as requested by the Hassricks—"detached from the [north-facing] living room, close to the boys' room in the back, and very clearly visible in the background when you [look] down the corridor. It will reflect rock garden and planting probably interestingly, illuminated at night."[36] In a letter to Neutra dated March 23, 1957, Barbara and Ken announced, "I think we've got it now!" giving their stamp of approval to the final scheme, labeled "Plan D."[37]

Once the design was finalized, construction of the house faced a number of challenges. Work was to start in March 1958, but was delayed as the Hassricks waited for their contractor, George Newman, to obtain a completion bond. There were also, apparently, many requests for clarification of the drawings, which may have delayed the project months, as suggested by Neutra's letter to Newman on April 14, 1958 when construction finally began.[38]

2.6 Hassrick House circa 1960. View to the northwest in the master bedroom. Thaddeus Longstreth Collection, The Architectural Archives, University of Pennsylvania. Photograph by Lawrence Williams.

2.7—2.8 Hassrick House circa 1960. Views to the west. The two story garage/bedroom addition designed by Neutra was built this year. Thaddeus Longstreth Collection, The Architectural Archives, University of Pennsylvania.

I was glad to answer all your questions and actually hear from yourself that you and all your sub-contractors have for sure asked us all questions for clarification and have no further doubts that everything as drawn and specified can be executed for the owners with proper results. This is what we and you are after with all our long, strenuous and expensive preparatory work..."[39]

Even so, the project did not run smoothly. Dealing with marital problems, Newman became less and less reliable; he eventually abandoned the project altogether and had moved to Florida by March 1959. Walter Hoinski, one of Newman's sub-contractors, stepped in to finish the house.[40] The Hassricks, who had already sold their Germantown house, were compelled to move in at Cherry Lane by February 1959, before it was finished.[41] Still, they were beyond pleased; Ken enthused that the house looked "'like a million dollars.'"[42]

Around this time Ken purchased a new Bugatti and wanted an enclosed garage to store it (the Neutra design only provided a carport). Thaddeus Longstreth responded by sending "some quick sketches" of a garage addition to Neutra for review. "They have asked us to show both a one story version which would not include the garage, necessitating their present carport being enclosed for the new Bugatti, and the two-story version with the garage on the lower level."[43] Neutra responded,

2.7

2.8

I would accept either solution; either the two-story or the one story solution. The garage door, the upper windows and the panel in between must become one panel for appearance if the two-story is used for the southeast elevation. A unified appearance of this two-story portion might make it an interesting accent of height.[44]

The two-story option was selected and built in 1960.[45] (Figures 2.7 and 2.8) The space adjacent to the kitchen had always been identified on drawings as the "Work Shop" for which the Hassricks had "plans for using it to complete interior details on the house or build furniture or some such."[46] Whether or not this space was also intended as an art studio for Ken is not known. What *is* known is that once the house was completed, Neutra was asked to design "a studio about 18' × 30' adjacent to the workshop" for Ken's use. The Hassricks were "a little surprised and chagrined" when

2.9

Neutra and Longstreth proposed a fee equal to 15% of the cost of construction for the design, "inasmuch as this job did not need too much in the way of drawings or attention and was a simple addition that they could settle for something [a] little less."[47] Ultimately, the Hassricks instead engaged a neighbor, young Philadelphia modernist architect, Irwin Stein, to design the studio addition, which was completed in 1961.[48]

Irwin J. (Jack) Stein (1930-) earned his architecture degree from the University of Pennsylvania, graduating in 1953. His early career was spent in the offices of notable Philadelphia architects designing in the mid-century modern style, including Oscar Stonorov and Frank Weise. Stein established his own practice in 1958. In contrast to Neutra's design, the addition by Stein had a traditional gable roof (with skylights). However, Stein did defer to Neutra's original concept, placing the addition on the back (west) side of the just completed garage addition where it would not be visible from the two principal house elevations, the front (east) and north sides. Stein's addition also created a courtyard with the south wall of the bedroom wing, and the west wall of the kitchen wing, an arrangement that might be seen as a nod to Neutra's theory of biorealism. The studio addition was further connected to the original house through the use of Bethayres block and the modernist preference for large continuous windows.[49]

Finally—the Hassrick House
Beginning in the 1940s, Neutra tempered his earlier, more industrial look, with warm tonalities in contrasts of textures and materials. In designing the Hassrick House, the architect employed design elements reflective of this evolving signature style, if at a more modest scale. The house features deep overhanging eaves, natural wood interior and exterior finishes, and floor-to-ceiling window walls to reduce perceived barriers between inside spaces and the outdoors. The plan follows a "pinwheel" arrangement anchored by the central core containing the principle living areas with short wings extending outward in all cardinal directions, a scheme reminiscent of Frank Lloyd Wright's Prairie Houses. Neutra's ability to adapt the design to the constraints of a limited budget owes a debt to the lessons of the Case Study House program and specifically Case Study House #20, the Bailey House, that presented similar financial challenges. (See Figure 1.6)

2.9 The Hassrick House circa 1960. View to the southwest. The front door to the house is behind the Bethayres block wall at center photo. Note the decorative Bethayres block wall at left photo, and the window wall in the living and dining area at right photo. Lawrence S. Williams Collection; Athenaeum of Philadelphia

2.10 Hassrick House circa 1960. View to the northeast from the kitchen area. Thaddeus Longstreth Collection, The Architectural Archives, University of Pennsylvania.

Approaching the house today from Cherry Lane, to the east, one is met by a blank wall of Bethayres block, behind which is the original carport. One "discovers" the front door by moving north and west around the carport, to the entry, which is covered by an open pergola and accented by a wall of Bethayres brick blocks with alternating running bond and saw-tooth masonry courses, a design element contributed by Longstreth. (Figure 2.9) The entrance is a narrow, low-ceiled foyer with a view to the north garden framed in such a way that the presence of the open space beyond is not initially perceived. Passing through the compressed space of the foyer, the panorama expands, opening to the primary living/dining/kitchen spaces, organized east to west along a striking forty-foot wall of floor-to-ceiling windows that blur boundaries and further interpenetrate spaces. This entry sequence and the volumetric interplay of compression and expansion is another move that recalls Wright, who often deployed the same dramatic spatial contrasts.

2.10

The bedroom "wings" are opposite the entry, on the west side of the house. From the foyer, the view to the west is through the living/dining area and down the bedroom corridor, through a window wall to the landscape beyond. Neutra anticipated that this view would eventually be toward a swimming pool, a near constant element of his residential designs which was never built as part of the Hassricks' plan. The original workshop, used variously by later occupants as a den or dining room, is up two steps, tucked behind the kitchen to the south, and now serves as an anteroom to the Stein addition. Neutra's pinwheel plan was established from the beginning, morphing in size and form as the architects and the Hassricks came to terms on the final plan and budget. The bedroom wing, which started as a long north-south corridor on the west side of the house, would become the current east-west corridor in the same location, with the master suite extending to the north to enclose the patio that opens from the living room/dining room/kitchen space at the heart of the house. (Figure 2.10)

The story of the emergence of the Hassrick House provides a snapshot of Neutra's design process, the reciprocal give-and-take between architect and clients, and his tireless efforts to tailor each house to its occupants. As Thaddeus Longstreth once promised the Hassricks, their house would exude the "beneficial physiological environment Mr. Neutra always creates."[50]

Drawings

Shannon McLain

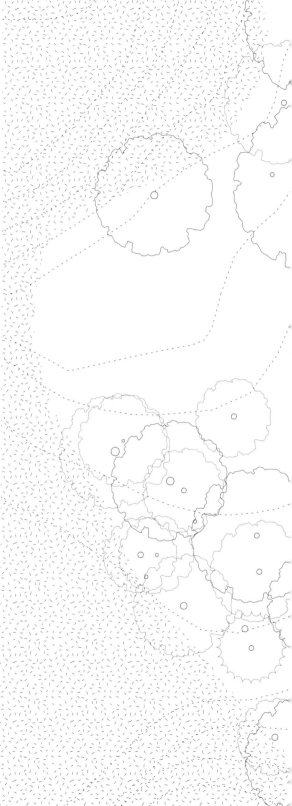

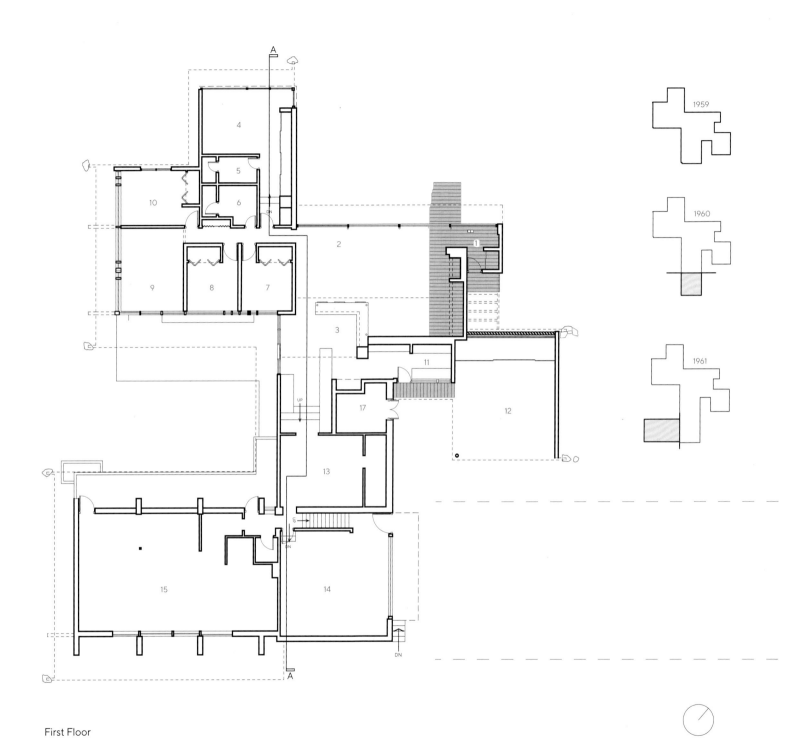

First Floor

1. Main Entry
2. Living Room
3. Kitchen
4. Master Bedroom (Original)
5. Master Bathroom
6. Bathroom
7. Bedroom
8. Bedroom
9. Playroom
10. Bedroom
11. Pantry / Secondary Entry
12. Carport
13. Studio (Original) / Dining Room
14. Garage (Neutra Addition)
15. Studio (Stein Addition)
16. Master Bedroom (Neutra Addition)
17. Mechanical

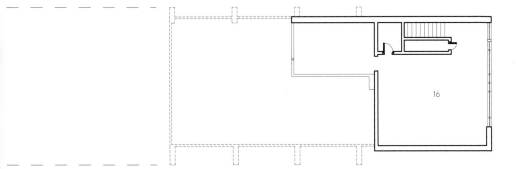

Second Floor

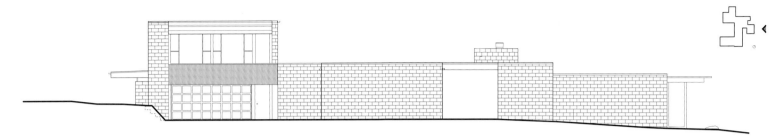

East Elevation

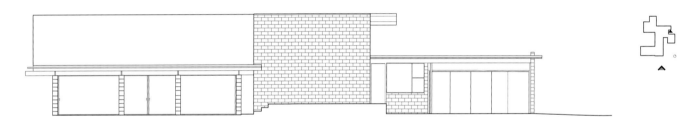

South Elevation

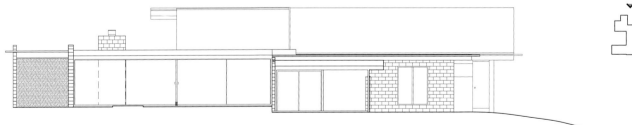

North Elevation

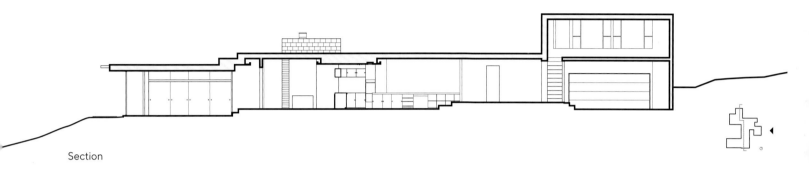

Section

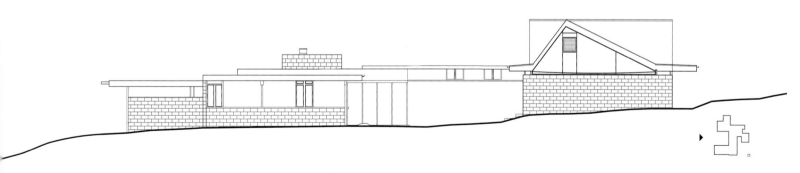

West Elevation

Hassrick House, perspective sketch by Richard Neutra, believed to
have been sent to Thaddeus Longstreth 3 March 1957, along with plan
options A, B and C. Courtesy Jonathan Sawyer.

CHAPTER 3

Neglect, Restoration, Reinvention

For all that they did to shape the house and its design, the Hassricks lived there for only four years. The family left the Philadelphia area and moved to Boulder, Colorado, in 1963, eventually moving further west, to Los Angeles, California, and then to southern Oregon where they raised Morgan horses and rare birds. Barbara and Ken ultimately settled in Whidbey Island, Washington, near their son, Matthew Hassrick, and his family.[1]

The house was sold to Henry and Grace Sawyer who lived there for nearly forty years. Henry Sawyer III attended the University of Pennsylvania and Penn Law (the University of Pennsylvania Law School), earning his law degree in 1948.[2] He married fellow Penn student Grace Scull in 1946. The Sawyers had three children: Jonathan, Henry (Hal), and Rebecca. Henry Sawyer III made his name as a civil liberties lawyer and is best known for his work in the Abington School District v. Schempp and the Lemon v. Kurtzman trials, both of which dealt with the division of church and state in public schools. In 1965, Sawyer became involved in the Civil Rights Movement when he traveled to Selma, Alabama, to help register Black voters. He served on the boards of many organizations, civic and otherwise, including the neighboring Philadelphia College of Textiles & Science, now Thomas Jefferson University.[3]

During the almost four decades of their occupancy, the Sawyers modified the original design in significant ways, customizing the house to accommodate the changing needs of their family and to satisfy their particular interests. Both Henry and Grace were avid gardeners and are

3.1

3.2

credited with planting many of the trees on the property. After removing Ken Hassick's foundry and welding equipment from the 1961 studio addition, the Sawyers transformed the space into an indoor greenhouse, replete with tropical plants and a floor to ceiling rubber tree. A thick rope attached by Henry to the studio's high ceiling served as a swing for the Sawyer children, allowing the greenhouse to double as a jungle gym. For a time, Grace Sawyer ran a needlepoint business out of the former studio.[4]

The couple built a pool at the northwest corner of the property, as the Hassricks had envisioned, but also constructed a roof deck over the master bedroom, accessible via a metal spiral staircase in the courtyard.[5] (Figure 3.1) To enlarge the space for their bedroom, and to move into a warmer part of the house, the Sawyers demolished the wall between the corner bedroom (originally Jonathan Fox's) and the sitting room/playroom. Also razed was a portion of the Bethayres Block wall to install new sliding glass doors to the exterior, allowing easy access to the pool from the relocated master suite.

The kitchen also underwent substantial reconfiguration by the Sawyers. The length of the peninsular counter, parallel to the courtyard, was shortened to make room for a detached island that was wider and taller than the original counters by several inches. Notably, they installed a permanent, fixed enclosure of walnut plywood in the opening between the suspended cabinets and the ceiling, walling off a distinctive feature of the original kitchen design. Moreover, Nakashima's sliding panels remained fully closed and stationary during the Sawyer era to protect guests in the dining area from being splashed by water from the sink—located in the adjacent counter—and to shield those seated on the built-in sofa in the living room from being splattered with hot grease from the facing stovetop. In effect, the Sawyers furthered the transition to a closed kitchen initiated by Barbara Hassrick, and administered the final blow to Neutra and Longstreth's design by turning the open kitchen into a closed-off room on three sides. The Sawyers attached a knife rack to the back of one of Nakashima's panels, underscoring its role as part of this permanent enclosure. Not surprisingly, in a visit to the house in the late 1960s, Neutra declared that the addition above the floating cabinets "looks terrible...like the bridge of a ship!"[6] (Figure 3.2)

The flat roof presented challenging drainage issues as Barbara Hassrick had predicted, resulting in standing pools of water and multiple leaks, exacerbated by inadequate gutters and a lack of downspouts. The Sawyers sought to alleviate these problems by superimposing a second, shallow-pitched, slanted roof above the original flat roof. To conceal the new gabled structure and maintain the rectangular silhouette of the house, a second fascia was added above the original, greatly increasing the height of this feature. Additional gutters were also installed, requiring the partial demolition of an original Bethayres Block parapet. As Hal Sawyer recalled, "My parents were not interested in architectural purity."[7]

The vicissitudes of family life impinged upon the original design in other ways. For privacy and noise reduction between children and adult areas, the uninterrupted flow of space through the hallway that connects the living room and playroom at each end was blocked with the addition of two doors—one at the threshold of the playroom and the other at the entrance to the living room. A third door was later erected mid-way between the two and positioned in the center of the hallway, providing a separation between the original master suite and children's wing. The forty-foot wide by nine-foot tall expanse of plate glass windows in the living area was at particular risk. Two sheets of glass were casualties when the family dog ran through one window and Hal shot a hole through another in a failed attempt to shoot an icicle off the roof. One replacement window is single paned plate glass that replicates the original material, while the other window was replaced with tempered glass that is now slightly warped and bows in the wind. Another incident capitalized on the indoor/outdoor permeability of the operable windows/doors. Hal Sawyer remembers his father would host his friends from the Americans for Democratic Action to listen to election returns. In 1968 when the television died and without a working radio, a guest drove his Karmann Ghia in through the sliding glass door, "two wheels on the slab-on-grade hearth, and two wheels on the floor frame and they listened to the returns on KYW News on the car radio."[8] (Figure 3.3)

When Henry and Grace Sawyer both died in 1999, Hal Sawyer and his wife Leila took ownership of the house and, after unsuccessful attempts to sell the property, lived there with their children between 2000 and 2002.[9] Hal removed "many of the fuzzy accretions my parents had added...the motel and mobile home feeling."[10] He dismantled the deteriorating roof deck, took down the spiral staircase and eliminated the wooden enclosure between the kitchen cabinets and ceiling, as well as the Plexiglass

3.3

3.1 Jonathan Sawyer constructing the roof deck over the master bedroom suite, circa 1963. Courtesy Jonathan Sawyer.

3.2 An unidentified group in the Sawyer's living room. Note the Nakashima panels, fixed in the closed position during the Sawyer residency, to separate the kitchen and living spaces. Courtesy Jonathan Sawyer.

3.3 In 1968 a friend of the Sawyers drove his Karmann Ghia into the living room so that they could listen to voting returns on the car radio. Courtesy Jonathan Sawyer.

3.4

3.5

3.6

storm windows and the multiple doors in the hallway. Hal also reproduced and reinstalled missing cabinet and closet doors.

After the Sawyers, the house went through three different owners over a period of six years. John McCoubrey, the president of Philadelphia-based construction firm McCoubrey/Overholser, and his wife Amy lived in the house from 2002 to 2006.[11] McCoubrey eliminated the pitched roof and additional fascia, reinstating the original flat roof. John Capoferri, a Philadelphia developer, owned the house for only two years until Earthstar Bank foreclosed on the property in March 2008. Concerned for its future, the Preservation Alliance for Greater Philadelphia listed the house in its *Fifth Annual Endangered Properties List* with the ominous sub-title, "Threatened, Still Threatened, and Threatened Again!"[12] (Figures 3.4–3.8)

Partners George Acosta and John Hauser had been frequent visitors to Palm Springs where they had long admired Neutra's Kaufmann Desert House. After relocating to Philadelphia, they were delighted to learn of a Neutra-designed residence for sale in the city. As Acosta recounted "... when I bought that house, people said I was crazy. I don't remember anyone saying that I had made a smart investment. But I dreamt about that house. I had been dreaming all my life for a house like that. I never actually thought I would live in one not to mention face the daunting task of restoring one from total dilapidation." When they first toured the house, it had been vacant for a number of years and had visibly, "fallen into heavy disrepair, like something out of Grey Gardens. ... Doors were unlocked and windows open. All sorts of animals were living inside."[13]

"...Regardless when we first walked up to it we looked at each other and both said, 'We are buying this house.' The asking price was very high, for the Philadelphia area, especially considering the condition. While on an out of town trip, we made an offer, but it was rejected, and we then contemplated a full-price counter. The thought of this home as a missed opportunity is what really motivated our decision, so we made financial arrangements for the purchase. When we returned to Philadelphia, we drove by on our way home from the airport. The For Sale sign was gone and all the doors had been secured with bolts and padlocks. Panicking, we called our agent, who discovered that the house had been foreclosed upon and was now owned by a local bank; the price had also been drastically reduced. After a roller coaster of obstacles, the home became ours. In fall 2008, we began the daunting task of bringing it back to life."[14]

In hindsight, George and John's purchase of the Hassrick house, and their concerted efforts to restore Neutra's original design, brought the story of the house full circle nearly 50 years after it was built. They were the first to see the house as an artifact and to take a studied approach to its restoration, undertaking in-depth research, obtaining documents from the Neutra and Longstreth archives at the University of California, Los Angeles and Penn Archives at the University of the Pennsylvania, respectively. Acosta eventually did much of the work himself, hiring craftspeople and learning from them so he could undertake restoration projects, a time consuming and challenging process. One particularly daunting task he recalled was restoring the tongue and groove clear cedar ceiling in the living room to its original high sheen, requiring him to refinish the surface multiple times.

Reinvention

In the words of George Acosta:

> So when I was offered the opportunity to participate in [the Jefferson] program…I jumped on it. At the time I had a feeling that I would be leaving Philadelphia soon… So I was beginning to see that with the university perhaps I could find a solution to my impending dilemma. Who will take care of everything I have done and continue to preserve this magical place. From there it all happened naturally…
>
> As I was going through all of this with this house, I continued to hear about Neutra buildings being torn down. So there was a sense of urgency for me to find a good custodian and it seemed to have landed in my lap as if meant to be. My interaction was constant with all of you [students]. It became a priority for me to assist all of you as much as needed…
>
> I wanted to tell my story of restoration on a budget. I wanted to communicate to anyone listening that these houses don't need to be so expensive to restore and my long term goal was to ultimately provide a resource for others who want to do the same thing.[15]

3.7

3.8

3.4 Hassrick House 2007. View to the east from the original dining area toward the living room fireplace wall. Courtesy Elizabeth Manning.

3.5 Hassrick House 2007. View to the east into the kitchen. Note the separate island at right foreground which dates to the Sawyer occupancy. Courtesy Elizabeth Manning.

3.6 Hassrick House 2007. View to the southwest from the main entrance toward the kitchen. Courtesy Elizabeth Manning.

3.7 Hassrick House 2007. View to the northeast into the Stein Addition. Courtesy Elizabeth Manning.

3.8. Hassrick House 2007. View to the northwest over the roof of the Stein Addition. Courtesy George Acosta and John Hauser.

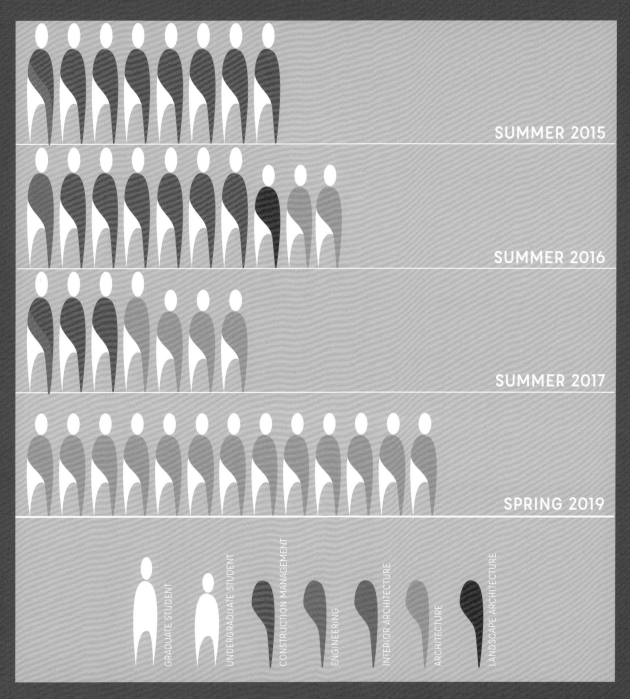

SUMMER 2015

SUMMER 2016

SUMMER 2017

SPRING 2019

GRADUATE STUDENT

UNDERGRADUATE STUDENT

CONSTRUCTION MANAGEMENT

ENGINEERING

INTERIOR ARCHITECTURE

ARCHITECTURE

LANDSCAPE ARCHITECTURE

2015–2019   STUDENT INVOLVEMENT

CHAPTER 4

Student Cohorts at the Hassrick House

George Acosta foresaw that, "...the students can be the future custodians" of the Hassrick House, and indeed, it has been the students who have taken the initiative to continue the stewardship of the house that was started back in 2015.[1] Senior and graduate students are training undergraduates to be docents so that this legacy program can continue to pass from class to class. A digital map of mid-century modern residences in the Delaware Valley is in progress, a cooperative effort with Docomomo Philadelphia. The Hassrick House provides an endless source of inspiration and study for the future professionals in the M.S. in Historic Preservation program. Their research and documentation of modern architecture, sparked by the Hassrick House, contribute to our ever-growing archive. It is hoped that just as the exhibit of 2019 inspired this book, this publication will inspire further study of Richard Neutra, Thaddeus Longstreth, and the Hassrick House, about which there is still much to be discovered. Here's to the next 50 years.

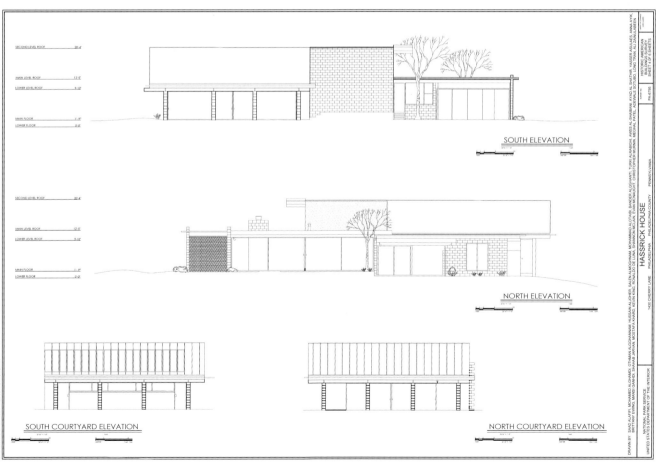

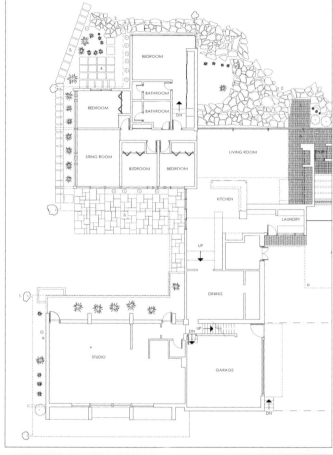

Monthly Cooling Load

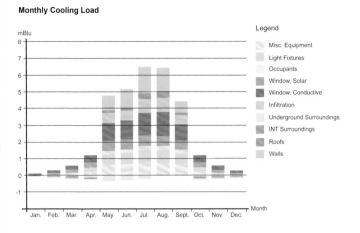

Legend

- Misc. Equipment
- Light Fixtures
- Occupants
- Window, Solar
- Window, Conductive
- Infiltration
- Underground Surroundings
- INT Surroundings
- Roofs
- Walls

HISTORIC AMERICAN BUILDINGS SURVEY

HASSRICK HOUSE

HABS No. PA-6795

Location:	4130 Cherry Lane, Philadelphia, Philadelphia County, Pennsylvania. A.K.A. 3033 West School House Lane, Philadelphia. Latitude: 40.022918 Longitude: -75.188984[1]
Present Owners:	Mr. John Hauser and Mr. George Acosta
Present Use:	Private Residence
Significance:	A carefully-restored example of Richard J. Neutra's work, the Hassrick House is an adaptation of typical features of Modernism, including floor-to-ceiling windows, overhanging eaves, and a strong spatial organization blending inside and outside, in a unique environment for the architect.

Coming at a time and place which were rapidly and thoroughly changing, it was no surprise that a style some saw as radical could take hold here. The "Philadelphia School" of architecture, design, and urban planning in the 1950s and 1960s included such well-known designers as Robert Venturi and Denise Scott Brown, Louis Kahn, Lewis Mumford, and Edmund Bacon and was focused on a functional approach to architecture, especially in the realm of urbanism. Jane Jacobs' seminal treatise, *The Death and Life of Great American Cities*, was published during this time, as was Kevin Lynch's *Image of the City*.[2]

December 18th, 1956

My dear Mr. Neutra:

    Before I get carried away with THE HOUSE, let me tell you how much we enjoyed meeting and talking with you. It was indeed a rare treat and a priviledge, and one that I hope we will repeat many times - as often, at least, as your schedule will permit.

    We are so convinced that your ideas of a home are also ours that we found that we kept saying "Oh, don't put that down, he knows." We don't want to build with the idea of impressing anyone (your name is enough to do that) we simply want a warm, friendly, gemutlich feeling expressed somehow in the clean fine style of good early Japanese. Ken says Zen. Is this possible? This is to say, the house must: 1/ work efficiently, 2/ pleasure the eye, 3/ comfort the soul, and 4/ warm the heart. My thought is that, while I don't hate housework, I hate thinking about it - I'd like it to move along so simply that my mind and eyes are free to enjoy the house.

    GENERAL EXTERIOR THOUGHTS: Pink Bethayers block we like very much. Idea: no wood siding at present to save $, but put it in design to be added later.

    Terraces: used brick, convenient to kitchen (sill-less door) also, if possible to bed-rooms and recreation room.

    Aluminum window frames and screens (Need I say)

    Trash yard convenient to kitchen.

    Flue tile garden wall somewhere.

    We would like a roof with a single pitch rather than flat top if not too many $ involved.

    Thought, would it be practical to put the shop, recreation room, wash room, and furnace in a semi basement, open on the woods side of the house, but underground on the street side.

    Radiant heat in floor.

    BEDROOMS: 3 about 10x16. 1 about 12x18. The master bedroom we would like to face the woods and open on terrace (bal-cony?)

    all small bedrooms should have walls that can be tacked on. Also, large sliding door storage walls for: hanging clothes, dresser drawers, bigger storage drawers, and desk space. We can figure out details later.

    Master bedroom, storage wall also - shoes, hanging clothes & drawers.

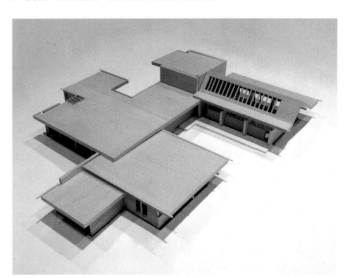

2015

Color Photographs
Hussain Aljoher

4.1

4.2

4.3

4.1–4.2 Previous pages. Views to the southwest.
4.3 View to the southwest.
4.4 View to the southeast.

4.4

4.5

4.5 Previous pages: View to the southwest
showing the original master suite.

4.6 View to the northeast showing the original
recreation room and boys bedroom wing.

4.6

4.7

4.8

4.9

4.10

4.7 Previous pages: View to the southwest from the living area toward the kitchen.

4.8 View to the west down the bedroom corridor from the dining area.

4.9 View to the southeast from the dining area to the living area.

4.10 View to the southwest in the original recreation room. The Stein Addition is visible through the windows at left photo.

4.11 Next pages: View to the northwest in the original master suite.

4.11

Student Engagement with the Hassrick House

Following is a list of all the students that have been involved with the Hassrick House since the first documentation efforts in 2015.

Key to Student Activities

Architectural Photography: Students documented the Hassrick House over time with digital and film photography.

Class Documentation: Students documented themselves, their classmates, and their processes of learning with the Hassrick House as a foundation for future students.

Documentation Drawings: Students started measuring and drawing the Hassrick House in 2015, an effort that culminated in the submission of a set of drawings to the Historic American Buildings Survey (HABS) collection in the Library of Congress.

Environmental Analysis: During the summer of 2017, students used energy analysis software, building information modeling (BIM), and FLIR thermal imaging cameras to survey the environmental performance of the Hassrick House. Student Long Tran led the effort to analyze the energy consumption of the house and provided recommendations, including payoff periods, to improve the overall performance and sustainability of the house.

Exhibit Design and Production: Students researched architectural exhibits, graphic design, and exhibit design to produce the Hassrick House Exhibit of April 8, 2019, showcasing their work from the Spring 2019 semester.

Historical Research: Research began with the HABS report, and continued through to 2019 when it was presented in the student-designed Hassrick House Exhibit on the occasion of the opening of the Center for the Preservation of Modernism on April 8, 2019.

Model Production: Raymond Bracy and Will Ferrill designed and constructed a wooden model of the house during the Spring 2019 semester and showcased it at the April 8, 2019 Hassrick House Exhibit.

Oral History Interviews: Students interviewed notable persons involved with the house, from former owners, like Hal Sawyer, to university faculty members that were involved with purchasing the building and using it as an educational tool.

Publication Production: Publications produced by students have been primarily independent studies using and showcasing student work and research.

Student Docent Program: Co-founders Anna Ayik and Alison Eberhardt analyzed existing historic sites with tour programs and established a docent guide to train student docents in 2019.

Student Docents: Volunteer student guides that are trained to give tours of the Hassrick House.

Tour Marshalls: Students who assisted in guiding guests through the Hassrick House as part of the April 8, 2019 Hassrick House Exhibit.

* = indicates a member of Students for Historic Preservation, a student-led campus organization founded in 2018 and dedicated to advocating for historic buildings on campus and in and around Philadelphia.

2015
ALI ZAINULABDEEN - Documentation Drawings (HABS)
AWS AL-SHAIBANI - Documentation Drawings (HABS)
AYAD ALSHATHIR - Documentation Drawings (HABS)
HUSSAIN ALJOHER – Architectural Photography, Documentation Drawings (HABS)
MEGHAL PATEL - Documentation Drawings (HABS)
MOHAMMAD ALOTAIBI - Documentation Drawings (HABS)
MOSTAFA KHARD - Documentation Drawings (HABS)
TURKI ALRABIGHI - Documentation Drawings (HABS)

2016
ANNA AYIK - Documentation Drawings (HABS), Class Documentation
BANDER ALQAHANTI - Documentation Drawings (HABS)
EVAN MCNAUGHT - Documentation Drawings (HABS), Landscape Survey
MANSI GANDHI - Documentation Drawings (HABS), Class Documentation, Interior Finishes Survey

MOHAMED ALGHAMDI - Documentation Drawings (HABS)
OTHMAN ALGGHANNAM - Documentation Drawings (HABS), Landscape Survey
SAAD ALARIFI - Documentation Drawings (HABS)
SALEH AL MOGHNAM - Documentation Drawings (HABS), Landscape Survey
SHAHAB JARVAN BAKHTIAN - Documentation Drawings (HABS)
SHANNON MCLAIN - Documentation Drawings (HABS), Class Documentation

2017

ADEWALE SOTUBO - Documentation Drawings (HABS), Environmental Analysis, Interior Finishes Survey
BRITTANY EWING - Documentation Drawings (HABS), Class Documentation
CHRISTOPHER MURNIN - Documentation Drawings (HABS)
KEVIN KING - Historical Research (HABS), Documentation Drawings (HABS)
RONALDO DE LUNA - Documentation Drawings (HABS), Class Documentation
LONG TRAN - Documentation Drawings (HABS), Environmental Analysis – Energy Audit
YASSER ASULAES - Documentation Drawings (HABS), Environmental Analysis

2019

ADAM HOOVER* - Historical Research, Student Docent, Exhibit Design and Production
ADRIANA HERNANDEZ PALOMINO* - Historical Research, Student Docent, Exhibit Design and Production
ALEX JONES* - Historical Research, Oral History Interviews, Student Docent, Exhibit Design and Production
ALISON EBERHARDT* - Historical Research, Student Docent Program Co-Founder, Student Docent, Architectural Photography, Exhibit Design and Production, Class Documentation
ANNA AYIK* - Documentation Drawings, Student Docent Program Co-Founder, Student Docent, Exhibit Design and Production
GRACE MESSNER* - Historical Research, Oral History Interviews, Student Docent, Exhibit Design and Production
HELEN PHAN* - Historical Research, Student Docent, Exhibit Design and Production

JESSICA RADOMSKI* - Historical Research, Oral History Interviews, Student Docent, Exhibit Design and Production
MADISON EMIG - Student Docent, Architectural Photography, Exhibit Design and Production
OLIVIA DEAGRO - Student Docent, Architectural Photography, Exhibit Design and Production, Class Documentation,
RAYMOND BRACY - Student Docent, Model Production, Exhibit Design and Production
SHANNON MCLAIN - Historical Research, Documentation Drawings, Student Docent, Exhibit Design and Production, Publication Production
THERESA CHIARENZA - Historical Research, Oral History Interviews, Student Docent, Exhibit Design and Production
WILL FERRILL - Student Docent, Model Production, Exhibit Design and Production
PATRICK KELLEY* – Tour Marshall
ONELL SANTIAGO* – Tour Marshall
WYATT ZIMMERMAN* – Tour Marshall
SPENCER RUBINO* – Tour Marshall
RILEY GARDINER* – Tour Marshall
ELIZABETH MAY* – Tour Marshall
DERECK SHERONY* – Tour Marshall
CHRIS CASSERLY* – Tour Marshall
DECLAN TORRENCE* – Tour Marshall

2020

ROSE DAVIS* – Architectural Photography
JESSICA RADOMSKI* – Lead Student Docent
ALISON EBERHARDT* – Graduate Assistant, Lead Student Docent, Publication Production
GRACE MESSNER* – Student Docent, Publication Production
ALEX JONES* – Student Docent

2021

ALISON EBERHARDT* – Graduate Assistant, Lead Student Docent, Publication Production
JESSICA RADOMSKI* – Young Adult Outreach, Publication Production, Lead Student Docent
ALEX JONES* – Student Docent

Endnotes

Introduction

1.   The date of construction is not known. The addition was completed sometime after November 1959, the date of the last known correspondence between Neutra and Longstreth regarding this addition. See Richard Neutra to Thaddeus Longstreth, 12 November 1959. Richard and Dion Neutra papers (LSC 1179). UCLA Library Special Collections, Charles E. Young Research Library, University of California, Los Angeles. All letters referenced are from the Richard and Dion Neutra papers (LSC 1179) UCLA Library Special Collections, unless noted otherwise.

2.   In a letter dated 9 May 1961, Longstreth informed Neutra that the Hassricks were "undertaking an addition to their studio and had already engaged another local architect." Thaddeus Longstreth to Richard Neutra, 9 May 1961.

3.   Drawings and a historical summary were accepted into the HABS collection in 2017. Library of Congress Prints and Photographs Division, Hassrick House, HABS No. PA-6795, https://www.loc.gov/pictures/item/pa4168/.

4.   From 2006-2008 the building was owned by a developer. During this two-year period, the house lay vacant and in poor condition until bank foreclosure. George Acosta and John Hauser purchased the house in 2008, saving the site from development and the house from possible demolition.

5.   Shannon McLain, Op-ed: Lessons Learned & Magic Found At Neutra's Hassrick House In East Falls, Hidden City, 4/30/2019. https://hiddencityphila.org/2019/04/op-ed-lessons-learned-magic-found-at-neutras-hassrick-house-in-east-falls/, accessed 5 May 2020.

6.   Shannon McLain interview with George Acosta and John Hauser, Philadelphia, PA, 26 March 2019.

Chapter 1

1.   Quoted in *TIME* magazine, 15 August 1949.

2.   Philip Johnson and Henry-Russell Hitchcock, *Modern Architecture: International Exhibition* (New York: Museum of Modern Art, 1932), 16.

3.   During the 1960s eight of Neutra's custom designed villas were constructed throughout Europe–four in Switzerland, three in Germany and one in France. These were preceded in 1959 by his glass encased U.S., Embassy building in Karachi, Pakistan. See Hubertus Adam, et.al., *Richard Neutra in Europa—Bauten und Projekte 1970-1970* (Cologne: Du Mont Buchverlag, 2010).

4.   *The Architecture of Social Concern* (1948) and *Survival by Design* (1954) are two of Neutra's most influential publications.

5.   Johnson and Hitchcock, 16.

6.   Lucinda Kaukas Havenhand, "Richard Neutra and the Modern Interior," *Mid-Century Modern Interiors, The Ideas that Shaped Interior Design in America* (New York, London, Oxford New Delhi, Sydney: Bloomsbury Visual Arts, 2019), 58.

7.   Neutra's studies were suspended temporarily when he served in the Viennese military. "Richard Joseph Neutra." *Encyclopedia Britannica*. 9 April 2018. https://www.britannica.com/biography/Richard-Joseph-Neutra, accessed 2 April 2019.

8.   Both Schindler and Neutra were influenced by the work of Frank Lloyd Wright, having seen Wright's Wasmuth portfolio on exhibit in Vienna in 1911.

9.   Harriet Roth, *Richard Neutra: The Story of the Berlin Houses, 1920-1924* (Berlin: Hatje Cantz, 2019).

10.   Arthur Drexler and Thomas S. Hine, *The Architecture of Richard Neutra: From International Style to California Modernism* (New York: The Museum of Modern Art, 1984), 8.

11.   This commission put the two former classmates at odds with one another. Schindler had designed the Lovell's previous house and believed Neutra stole the commission from him. Havenhand, 39.

12.   "The Lovell House is claimed to be the first house in the United States to use a steel structure that is typically found in skyscraper construction – Neutra learned these new techniques when he was working in New York and with Holabird & Roche in Chicago." Andrew Kroll. "AD Classics: Lovell House / Richard Neutra" 18 January 2011. *ArchDaily*. Accessed 13 April 2020. <https://www.archdaily.com/104713/ad-classics-lovell-house-richard-neutra/> ISSN 0719-8884.

13.   Alfred H. Barr, Jr. in the Forward to, *Modern Architecture: International Exhibition,* (New York: Museum of Modern Art, 1932), 13.

14.   Richard Neutra, *Survival by Design* (New York: Oxford University Press, 1954), 195.

15.   Neutra was a childhood friend of Ernst, Sigmund Freud's son, and as an adult, he maintained contact with Freud and interest in his theory of psychoanalysis. See Havenhand, 36.

16.   For analysis of Neutra's philosophy of biorealism, see Havenhand, 35-59 and Maarten Overdijk, "Richard Neutra's Therapeutic Architecture," *FA Failed Architecture,* Accessed 14 February 2021. failedarchitecture.com/richard-neutras-therapeutic-architecture/.

17.   Richard Neutra, "Case Study House #20," *Art and Architecture*, (December 1948): 32-41 and 56.

18.   Neutra, "Case Study House #20," 36.

19.   Neutra, "Case Study House #20," 38.

20.   Thomas Hine, *Richard Neutra and the Search for Modern Architecture: A Biography and History* (New York: Oxford University Press, 1982), p. 211.

Chapter 2

1.   Barbara Hassrick to Richard Neutra, 18 December 1956. Richard and Dion Neutra papers (LSC 1179). UCLA Library Special Collections,

Charles E. Young Research Library, University of California, Los Angeles. All letters referenced are from the UCLA Archive. All letters referenced are from the Richard and Dion Neutra papers (LSC 1179) UCLA Library Special Collections, unless noted otherwise.

2. John Hauser, "Three Acres & a Bugatti," *Atomic Ranch* (Winter 2013): 34. Richard Neutra appeared on the cover of the 15 August 1949 issue of *TIME* magazine.

3. *The Philadelphia Inquirer,* 9 April 1956.

4. As Thaddeus Longstreth explained to the Hassricks, Neutra "asked me to request from you if possible photographs of the members of your family. The purpose of this request is so that not only he [Neutra] but his entire staff feel a close personal relationship in each phase of the design to those for whom the design is intended. Also would you please send to him the names and ages of your children, identifying them on the back of the photographs." Thaddeus Longstreth to Barbara and Ken Hassrick, 21 February 1957.

5. Lucinda Kaukas Havenhand, "Richard Neutra and the Modern Interior," *Mid-Century Modern Interiors, The Ideas that Shaped Interior Design in America* (New York, London, Oxford New Delhi, Sydney: Bloomsbury Visual Arts, 2019), 57.

6. Barbara Hassrick was sometimes called Doll or Dolly.

7. The couple had two children, Jonathan and Jeremy. Barbara and Ken Hassrick had one son, Matthew.

8. See for example, "Hassrick Exhibit," *The Philadelphia Inquirer,* 20 May 1962, 8.

9. "Stilled, but not stopped," *South Whidbey Record,* 18 June 2003. https://www.southwhidbeyrecord.com/news/stilled-but-not-stopped/, accessed 3 June 2020.

10. The Cohen Residence (1954, https://www.philadelphiabuildings. org/pab/app/pj_display.cfm/47997) and the Miller Residence (1955, https://www.philadelphiabuildings.org/pab/app/pj_display.cfm/48808). It's possible the Hassricks or the Estabrooks knew the Cohens. Correspondence confirms that there was no connection between the Hassricks and the Millers. "After the holidays and when Mrs. Miller is settled I will arrange for them [the Hassricks] to see that house." Thaddeus Longstreth to Richard Neutra, 17 December 1956.

11. Emily Cooperman, Bibliography: Longstreth, Thaddeus (1909-1997), Architect, Philadelphia Architects and Buildings, https://www. philadelphiabuildings.org/pab/app/ar_display.cfm/22922, accessed 24 April 2020.

12. Thaddeus Longstreth's letterhead identified him as "Architect and Consultant." See for example, Thaddeus Longstreth to Richard Neutra, 12 June 1957.

13. Either the Hassricks asked or Neutra offered, references: "As promised, I shall have my office enclose at random some letters of clients, whom we satisfied over long distance by our careful work; we have so many of these letters." Richard Neutra to Barbara and Ken Hassrick, 12 December 1956.

14. On one Hassrick House design development drawing Neutra noted, "Beds at windows in this climate bad! Millers are not happy about it." R. Neutra, "Residence for: Mr. and Mrs. K. Hassrick," Thaddeus Longstreth Collection, The Architectural Archives, University of Pennsylvania.

15. The Hassricks mailed a retainer fee to employ Neutra and "their lists that you asked them to prepare" implying that Neutra requested their input and requirements for the house. Thaddeus Longstreth to Richard Neutra, 17 December 1956.

16. Because the Hassrick's had a relatively modest budget of $30,000, some aspects of the design, such as finishes, were planned for completion at a later date. Accounting for inflation, $30,000 is the equivalent of approximately $283,000 in 2020 (CPI Inflation Calculator, https://www.in2013dollars.com/us/inflation/1956?amount=30000, accessed 1 June 2020).

17. Barbara and Ken Hassrick to Richard Neutra, 18 December 1956.

18. Barbara and Ken Hassrick to Richard Neutra, 18 December 1956.

19. Barbara and Ken Hassrick to Richard Neutra, 4 January 1957.

20. Barbara and Ken Hassrick to Richard Neutra, 18 December, 1956.

21. Thaddeus Longstreth to Richard Neutra, 8 March, 1857.

22. Thaddeus Longstreth to Richard Neutra, 8 March, 1957. In a letter from Longstreth to Neutra dated 12 June 1957, Longstreth wrote, "In regard to the kitchen cabinets facing the living area, they wanted them free standing with open space above them so as to see the ceiling going thru over them. This seems quite feasible by introducing a second pipe column at the west end of the cabinets for additional support (this will help our framing too). They would like wood counter tops in the kitchen."

23. Barbara Hassrick to Richard Neutra, 4 January 1957.

24. Nakashima Invoice, 28 February 1959. Nakashima is renowned for his handcrafted furniture that celebrates the natural characteristics of materials, primarily wood.

25. Barbara Hassrick to Thaddeus Longstreth, n.d. (c. 1 April 1961). Neutra's response was not unexpected: "I am not too delighted about these heavily framed panels, but I suppose and hope they could be removed when a photograph is being taken…" Richard Neutra to Thaddeus Longstreth, 4 April 1961.

26. Richard Neutra to Barbara and Ken Hassrick, 14 January 1957.

27. Barbara Hassrick to Richard Neutra, 5 February 1957.

28. Barbara Hassrick wrote that she "is surprised that you ask about postponing the shop—I think that hardly a letter has gone out from me that doesn't mention our plans for using it to complete interior details on the house or building furniture of some such… I was under the impression that we could build what we wanted for what we had to spend…I didn't think that we'd have to chop off such large and important features." Barbara Hassrick to Richard Neutra, 26 February 1957.

29. Richard Neutra to Thaddeus Longstreth, 3 March 1957.

30. Thaddeus Longstreth to Richard Neutra, 5 March 1957.

31. Barbara Hassrick to Richard Neutra, 2 February 1957 and 12 February 1957, and Thaddeus Longstreth to Barbara Hassrick, 16 February 1957.

32. Thaddeus Longstreth to Richard Neutra, 23 May 1957. On the Hassricks' ownership of monkeys see, "Zoo in the Home: Starting out to buy a car, they wound up with a monkey," *The Philadelphia Inquirer Magazine*, 16 December 1956, 11.

33. Richard Neutra to Mr. and Mrs. Hassrick, 9 February 1957.

34. Richard Neutra to Thaddeus Longstreth, 3 March 1957.

35. Thaddeus Longstreth to Richard Neutra, 8 March 1957.

36. Richard Neutra to Thaddeus Longstreth, 13 March 1957.

37. Barbara and Ken Hassrick to Richard J. Neutra, 23 March 1957.

38. Richard Neutra to Barbara and Ken Hassrick, 11 September 1958.

39. Richard J. Neutra to George W. Newman, 14 April 1958.

40. Walter Hoinski was low bidder on another Neutra project, the Seitchik Residence. Thaddeus Longstreth to Richard Neutra, 27 March 1959.

41. Concerning the Hassricks, they moved in several months early because they had to give up their old house to the new owners. "George Newman has not finished many little odds and ends. His wife is divorcing him. ... The Hassricks have finished the chimney as well as many other things their own way, the cabinet work particularly, and since the monkey died and there is no longer need for a cage, that area of the house is a 'no-man's-land.'" Thaddeus Longstreth to Richard Neutra, 21 February 1959. Longstreth earlier reported: "They are also going to plaster the west face of the fireplace and Ken wants to paint a mural on this area which he said you would not object! He seemed fairly set with this idea and with leaving exposed the four inch block so I thought I had better advise you who have much greater influence over him." Thaddeus Longstreth to Richard Neutra, 17 November 1958.

42. Thaddeus Longstreth to Richard Neutra, 8 August 1959.

43. Thaddeus Longstreth to Richard J. Neutra, 17 October 1959.

44. Richard J. Neutra to Thaddeus Longstreth, 19 October 1959.

45. This correspondence illustrates the fluid working relationship between Neutra and Longstreth, which is worthy of further study.

46. Barbara Hassrick to Richard J. Neutra, 26 February 1957. They were an artistic family. Barbara's sons from her first marriage, Jonathan and Jeremy Fox, would help Ken in the garage or in his studio. Matthew Hassrick was building sculptures from the age of four. Barbara Hassrick shot and developed her own film in a dark room in the house.

47. Thaddeus Longstreth to Richard Neutra, 12 November 1959.

48. "I am sorry to report that on my last visit to the Hassricks I found that they are undertaking an addition to their studio and had already engaged another local architect who had made some drwgs for them. I will check to see if work has commenced on this yet. Their planting is very beautiful." Thaddeus Longstreth to Richard J. Neutra, 9 May 1961.

After all the design modifications to reduce costs for the house, how it was that the garage and studio additions were proposed as construction of the house was being completed is not clear.

49. Stein's addition did, however, foil Neutra's plan for the view to a future pool from the front entry west to the full height windows on the west wall of the original playroom.

50. Thaddeus Longstreth to Barbara and Ken Hassrick, 16 February 1957.

Chapter 3

1. Iona Miller, *Ken Hassrick – Avant-Garde Sculptor & Painter – 'The Body Electric,' My Art Mentors, Collaborators & Artistic Inspirations,* website, https://ionamiller.weebly.com/artistic-inspirations.html, accessed 3 June 2020.

2. Henry Sawyer III had been engaged to Barbara Estabrook (Hassrick) but the engagement broke off when Sawyer was deployed for WWII. The primary source of information about the Sawyer era is Hal Sawyer, "Growing up in Mr. Neutra's House," for the archives of Philadelphia University, formerly The College of Textiles and Science (now Thomas Jefferson University), 2019, 1-30.

3. In 1965, while serving as president of the southeastern Pennsylvania chapter of the Americans for Democratic Action, Sawyer led a group of Democrats who endorsed Arlen Specter for district attorney of Philadelphia.

4. Sawyer, 14.

5. The deck was built by Jonathan Sawyer, a carpenter.

6. Sawyer, 9.

7. Sawyer, 19.

8. Sawyer, 15.

9. Hal Sawyer, Interview by Theresa Chiarenza and Grace Messner, 30 March 2019.

10. Sawyer, 24.

11. It was while the McCoubreys owned the house that the film, *Happy Tears*, featuring Demi Moore, was filmed there.

12. Preservation Alliance for Greater Philadelphia, *Fifth Annual Endangered Properties List*, Preservation Matters, Winter 2007, p. 3, www.preservationalliance.com/files/winter2008, accessed 3 August 2020.

13. John Hauser, "Three Acres & a Bugatti," *Atomic Ranch*, Winter 2013, 35.

14. John Hauser, "Three Acres & a Bugatti," *Atomic Ranch*, Winter 2013, 35.

15. George Acosta, Interview with Shannon McLain, 2019.

Chapter 4

1. Interview with George Acosta and John Hauser, Philadelphia, PA, 26 March 2019.